Rodrigo Ferreira Gonçalves

Implementing a Failover Cluster using Proprietary Software

Rodrigo Ferreira Gonçalves

Implementing a Failover Cluster using Proprietary Software

Failover de cluster

ScienciaScripts

Imprint
Any brand names and product names mentioned in this book are subject to trademark, brand or patent protection and are trademarks or registered trademarks of their respective holders. The use of brand names, product names, common names, trade names, product descriptions etc. even without a particular marking in this work is in no way to be construed to mean that such names may be regarded as unrestricted in respect of trademark and brand protection legislation and could thus be used by anyone.

Cover image: www.ingimage.com

This book is a translation from the original published under ISBN 978-613-9-60279-7.

Publisher:
Sciencia Scripts
is a trademark of
Dodo Books Indian Ocean Ltd. and OmniScriptum S.R.L publishing group

120 High Road, East Finchley, London, N2 9ED, United Kingdom
Str. Armeneasca 28/1, office 1, Chisinau MD-2012, Republic of Moldova, Europe
Printed at: see last page
ISBN: 978-620-7-27352-2

ACKNOWLEDGEMENTS

I would like to thank my parents, who, throughout this journey, have given me strength and family life, which has been very important for me to carry out my efforts in the specialisation and to be able to prepare myself to face a new professional reality. To all the professors at the Postgraduate Programme in Distributed Systems with an Emphasis on Databases at the Federal University of Pampa - UNIPAMPA, for sharing their vast knowledge and especially to my supervisor and co-supervisor, Prof. Carlos Michel Betemps and Prof. Sandro da Silva Camargo, for accepting, believing in and guiding this work and also to my fellow students for their friendship and companionship and especially to God for giving me the strength and courage to carry out this work.

"Whoever you are, whatever position you have in life, at the highest or lowest social level. Always aim for a lot of strength, a lot of determination and always do everything with a lot of love and a lot of faith in God, that one day you'll get there, somehow you'll get there."

Ayrton Senna

SUMMARY

Providing services without interruption is a critical requirement, as failure can cause financial damage to the company as well as its reputation. In view of this scenario, the aim of this work was to implement a High Availability solution using proprietary *software.* In this context, it was hypothesised that the implementation of a *Failover Cluster* would guarantee the High Availability of the information distributed among the servers. The methodology used to achieve the aim of this work was to review the literature on the subject. As a result, it was possible to make adjustments to the *Cluster* configurations. It was concluded that the servers that took part in the implementation responded to the majority of the tests applied, thus guaranteeing the High Availability of the information.

Keywords: *Failover Cluster*; Implementation; High Availability.

SUMMARY

CHAPTER 1

INTRODUCTION

Nowadays, due to the need to meet different business requirements, many organisations are migrating their corporate systems from the local network environment to the *web* environment. In this new reality, providing services without interruption is a critical requirement, as a failure can be significant both in terms of generating short-term financial impacts and long-term damage to corporate reputation (ZHANG, ABDELZAHER, STANKOVIC, 2004).

A viable solution for increasing service availability is to use *clusters, so that* when one node fails, control is transferred to another, so that the service continues to be offered even when one node fails.

Clusters emerged with the aim of overcoming some of the difficulties of centralised systems and also to increase the performance of standardised applications, networks and tools for high-performance distributed computing. Their emergence has necessitated some changes in application development, due to the tendency for applications to be built to run in decentralised environments. The composition of a *cluster* covers complex computing research issues such as scalability, availability, fault tolerance and high performance (ALECRIM, 2013).

In order to make the failure unnoticeable to the *cluster* user, the *failover* technique allows requests to be redirected to another node. In the database context, a *Failover Cluster* is useful if a node fails, or if there is any planned maintenance on the Database System resources (ASWINI, MANISANKAR, JAGADEESAN, 2012).

The main technological achievements of the 20th century have been in the field of acquiring, processing and distributing information. With the advance of these technologies, the time spent collecting, processing, distributing and analysing data has become invisible to users. Technological solutions have evolved, high availability techniques have emerged and *clusters* can offer scalability and availability of resources, services and applications (TANEBAUM, 2003).

1.1 RESEARCH PROBLEM

With technological and economic advances, many companies increasingly need to handle information securely and continuously. To do this, they need servers that can make stored data available to users quickly and efficiently. In this context, will the implementation of a *Failover Cluster* guarantee the High Availability of resources and applications, leaving this information distributed among the servers?

1.2 BACKGROUND

The motivation behind this work is the relevance of the topic for organisations that use information systems for data management. This implementation will be important for the researcher, as the knowledge gained from the work will add value to his professional and academic life.

The implementation of the *Failover Cluster* will offer several improvements in terms of High Availability and Scalability of resources. It will also provide fault-tolerant mechanisms, with the ability to add new resources or replace existing ones, as such changes will not be noticeable to users.

1.3 OBJECTIVES

1.3.1 **General Objective**:

Implement a high availability solution using proprietary *software.*

1.3.2 **Specific Objectives:**

- Carry out a literature search on approaches and resources for implementing high availability;
- Provide details of the methodology in this work;
- Describe the proposed implementation environment;
- Implementing *Cluster Failover* on the servers;
- Apply implementations and configurations to the systems that will be part of the *cluster*;
- Validate the implementation of the *cluster* with performance analysis tools;
- Simulate server connection failure after implementation;
- Test the performance of the systems;
- Show the results obtained from the experiments carried out.

1.4 METHODOLOGY

A bibliographical survey was carried out in order to obtain the theoretical background needed to understand the aspects related to implementation.

The procedure used consists of a scientific study of a specific topic, with the aim of obtaining generalisations. The monograph presented the factors that constituted and influenced the implementations applied.

This study used the bibliographical or secondary source technique, which aims to collect and collate information in order to choose and study a series of authors who cover the topic of interest to the researcher.

This work describes the implementation of a *Failover Cluster,* which was applied as follows:

Theme definition: Where the theme and the form of implementation were decided, based on bibliographical research.

Analysis phase: An analysis was made of how the *Failover Cluster* implementation would distribute the data between the servers.

Implementation: In this phase the resources on the servers were installed and configured, as well as the *software* installations and computer configurations.

Tests: At this point the tests were carried out to obtain the results of the applications, where all the development part of this study was commented on.

1.5 WORK STRUCTURE

This work is organised into seven chapters, the contents of which are structured in an attempt to provide a clear and concise overview of various issues that are pertinent to understanding the main proposal set out here, which relate content of significant importance for carrying out the data analysis.

Chapters two, three and four are made up of the Bibliographical Review, which contains all the material researched for the development of this work, as well as topics relating to Databases, Data Replication, Reliability, Redundancy and Types of *Clusters*. Chapter five describes the process of developing the work, involving the Implementation Techniques and the Description of the Implemented *Cluster*. Chapter six shows the tests carried out with the Experiments and Data Collected. Chapter seven presents the conclusions of this work and proposals for future work.

CHAPTER 2

LITERATURE REVIEW

Bibliographical research provides a wide range of information, as well as enabling the use of data scattered throughout numerous publications. The topics chosen below helped to construct the results and conclusions of the object proposed in this study.

2.1 DATABASE

According to Melo (2004), databases are a collection of logically interrelated and coherent data with some inherent meaning. According to the same author, a database is designed, built and populated with data for a specific purpose, has pre-conceived applications and aims to serve a certain group of users. Its aim is to provide a unique, non-redundant and strictly scaled representation of an application's data.

Relational databases organise their data in tables, which are structured by rows, called tuples, and columns, called fields. A *Database Management System (*DBMS), on the other hand, is special *software* that allows data to be controlled in one place, making it available to various applications.

The DBMS serves as an interface between the common database and the various application programmes. DBMSs overcome many of the limitations of traditional file environments:

S The data is independent of the application programmes;

S Data redundancy and inconsistency are reduced;

S Database complexity is reduced by consolidated data management;

S Information is easier to access and use (LAUDON, 2004).

2.2 DATABASE SYSTEM ARCHITECTURES

The architecture of a Database System is divided into three levels, known as the internal level, the conceptual level and the external level.

Generally speaking, the internal level, also known as the physical level, is closest to the physical storage medium, i.e. it is concerned with how the data is physically stored. The external level, also known as the logical user level, is closest to the users and deals with how the data is seen by individual users. The conceptual level, also known as the community logic level or indirect unqualified level, is a simulation level, i.e. it is a process of designing a computer model of a real system and conducting experiments with this model in order to understand its behaviour and/or evaluate strategies for its operation (DATE, 2004).

2.3 DATA COMMUNICATION

Requests to an end user's database are transmitted from the user's workstation, which may be physically far from the database system itself, to an available application (*online), whether* embedded or not, to the DBMS, in the form of communication messages.

Similarly, responses from the DBMS and the application to the user's workstation are also transmitted in the form of messages. All these message transmissions take place under the control of another *software* component, the DC (*Data Communications*) manager.

The DC manager is not part of the DBMS, but is an autonomous system. However, as the DC manager and the DBMS are clearly required to work in harmony, the two are sometimes considered equal partners in a higher-level co-operative venture called the Database/Data Communications System (DB/DC System). The DBMS takes care of the database and the DC manager handles all messages to and from the DBMS or, more precisely, to and from applications that use the DBMS (DATE, 2004).

This chapter has dealt with database topics, an essential subject for continuing the study, as well as providing a basis for understanding how the redundancy mechanisms applied in this implementation work, a subject that will be covered in the next chapter.

CHAPTER 3

CONCEPTS ASSOCIATED WITH FAULT TOLERANCE

Chapter 3 aims to present the main concepts of Redundancy, Information Redundancy, Temporal Redundancy, *Hardware Redundancy, Software* Redundancy, Reliability, Data Replication and Replication Types in *Microsoft SQL Server* 2008.

3.1 REDUNDANCY

Redundancy can exist in various components, such as power supplies, network interfaces, processors, communication *links* and servers. Redundancy is an important practice for mission-critical systems, because if one component fails, the system continues to function normally.

A very clear example is computer network equipment such as *hubs*, *switches* and *routers*, which are currently the peripherals built with the redundancy solution. Redundancy is used to implement fault tolerance techniques and can be applied in various ways (WEBER, 2002).

3.2 REDUNDANT INFORMATION

According to Weber (2002), this type of redundancy uses a coding technique for error detection or fault masking. In this redundancy model, the extra bits or signals are stored or transmitted along with the data, without containing any useful information.

There are some examples of information redundancy such as parity codes, where n+1 bits are stored for every *n* bits. The extra bit is only used to indicate whether the number of data bits with a value of 1 is even or odd.

It also makes it possible to detect single-bit faults, i.e. faults that only affect 1 bit of a word. Another clear example of codes used to check for errors are the *Hamming Code* and *Cyclic Redundancy Codes* (CRC). In the Hamming Code model, multiple parity bits are added to the data, each associated with a subset of bits.

Cyclic codes are codes applied to blocks of data, sequences of bits associated with polynomials. By using a generator polynomial of degree x to calculate the extra bits, it is possible to detect sequences of erroneous bits with a length less than x.

3.3 TEMPORAL REDUNDANCY

This type of redundancy uses time to implement a given function designed to detect or tolerate faults, where this function can be implemented in the form of repeating calculations, comparing results, repeating message sending or comparing values.

In systems where time is not critical or the processor has idle time, it can be used to detect transient *hardware* faults.

There are two common applications of time redundancy:

1ª Application: Transient fault detection: Repeat processing. The existence of distinct and different results is a very strong indication of a transient fault.

2nd Application: Permanent fault detection: This model repeats the computation with the encoded information and decodes the information before comparing it with the previous result (WEBER, 1990, 2002).

3.4 *HARDWARE* REDUNDANCY

Hardware redundancy is based on the replication of physical components. Categorised into:

- **Passive *Hardware* Redundancy**

In this type, redundant components are used to mask faults, i.e. they correct errors without involving system actions. All the elements perform the same activities and the result is determined by voting, which is *Triple Modular Redundancy* (TMR).

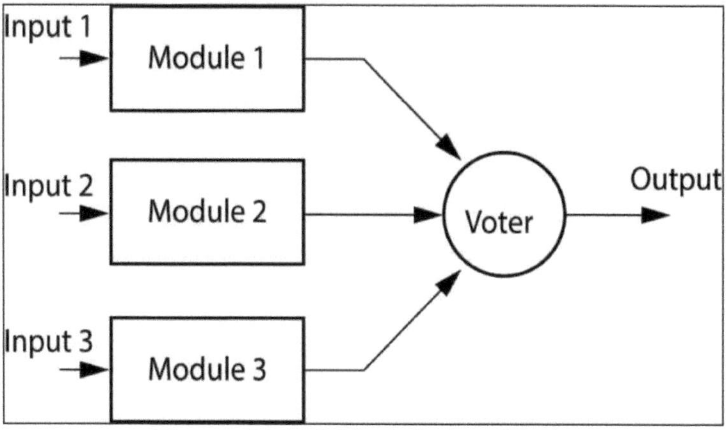

Figure 1: *Triple Modular Redundancy* (TMR).

Source: (http://hpc.ee.kmutnb.ac.th/~vara/perf/node132.html).

According to Shoman (2002), the system shown in figure 1 consists of three modules: module 1, module 2 and module 3, all with the same output. The results of the three modules are compared by the voting element (*Voter*), which checks and gives its opinion of the system's output. If all three modules are operating correctly, all the results are the same, so the system's output is correct. However, an important observation is when the output is not unique, i.e. when there is more than one *output,* because this reduces the fragility of the *voter* and increases the reliability of the operation.

- **Active *Hardware* Redundancy**

This redundancy has several processing elements, but only one works at a time, the others are supplements. If a fault is found in an operating unit, then it is removed and replaced by a spare via a "*switching*" circuit [interconnection of two or more circuits].

It is used in applications that support remaining in an erroneous state for a certain period of time, where this time is sufficient for error detection and recovery to a fault-free state. This type of redundancy requires error detection, diagnosis and reconfiguration.

3.5 *SOFTWARE* REDUNDANCY

According to Weber (2002), one of the ways of guaranteeing *software* redundancy, without the occurrence of errors, is the use of independent *software* versions [obviously making the cost higher], not using the hypothesis that independent programming groups will incorporate *software* errors into the same (common mode), degrading the amount of redundancy provided.

There are other ways of applying *software* redundancy to detect faults and mask faults that do not use the same *software* copy, which are Diversity and Recovery Blocks.

Diversity is a redundancy technique used to achieve diversified programming ("n" versions), i.e. several implementation alternatives are developed. Therefore, in the testing phase, possible errors can be located and corrected. You can then opt for the alternative in which the fewest errors have been detected.

The Recovery Blocks technique uses acceptance testing, i.e. programmes are executed and tested one by one until the first one passes the acceptance test. In this way, secondary programmes are only needed if an error is detected in the primary programme.

3.6 RELIABILITY

According to Vollertt (1996), reliability is a function that represents the probability of a system being operational or not:

- **Operating Status at the Start of the Period**

  It's a basic premise, because you can't talk about reliability in systems that start out faulty.

- **Specification**

  To know whether a system is reliable or not, you need to have a specification of how it should work. We can take a bridge as an example: it must have a specification for how many tonnes of weight it can support, in order to prevent a lorry with a very heavy load from trying to cross and the bridge collapsing.

- **Defined conditions**

  Conditions such as room temperature and humidity must be known in order for the system to work properly.

- **Period of Operation**

The time the system will be up and running must be known. In the case of the bridge, assuming that it is elevated and can only be used from 6am to 6pm, then it should be specified that from 6pm to 6am it will be unavailable, not because a problem has occurred, but because of issues related to the specification.

3.7 DATA REPLICATION

According to Freitas (2003), Data Replication is used to increase data availability. There are cases where it will be necessary to replicate all the Databases within the transaction, creating a fully replicated Distributed Database, thus generating characteristics such as Availability, Increased Parallelism and Increased Update *Overhead.*

- **Availability**: If a node (network access point) that contains a relation "x" fails, consequently this relation can be found on another node. Thus, the system will be able to continue processing queries involving the "x" relation, despite the failure of a node.
- **Increased** Parallelism: Several nodes can process queries in parallel on "x". The more replicas of "x" there are, the greater the chance that the necessary data will be found on the node where the transaction is being executed. Therefore, data replication minimises the movement of data between nodes.
- **Increased Update *Overhead***: The system must ensure that all replicas of a relation "x" are consistent, otherwise erroneous processing can occur. Thus, every time "x" is updated, the update must be propagated to all nodes that contain replicas. The result is an increased *overhead.*

3.8 DATABASE REPLICATION

According to Silberschatz and Karth (1991), the purpose of a data replication mechanism is to allow several identical copies of the same data to be maintained in various database management systems. Database replication can take two forms:

- **Synchronous Replication**: All copies or replications of data will be made at the moment of synchronisation and consistency. If any copy of the bank is changed, this change will be immediately applied to all the other banks within the transaction. Synchronous Replication is appropriate in commercial applications where the exact consistency of information is of the utmost importance.

- **Asynchronous Replication:** Stores and replicates. At first, the copy of the data is out of sync between the databases; if any data is changed, the modification will be propagated and applied to another database. At a second moment, within a separate transaction (which could take place seconds, minutes, hours or even days later, with the copies temporarily out of sync), synchronisation will take place and the data will go to all the specified locations.

Both types of replication can be used. Synchronous replication will be used when each transaction is considered complete, i.e. when all nodes confirm that the local transaction was successful. Asynchronous replication will be used when a node executes the transaction and sends the confirmation to the requester and then forwards the transaction to the other nodes.

3.9 TYPES OF REPLICATION IN *MICROSOFT SQL SERVER* 2008

According to Lopes (2013), when a *Database* server is enabled for Replication, it will request the creation of a new System Database, which will act as a repository for information about the publications created. This *Database* is called a Distributor.

Microsoft SQL Server 2008 supports the following replications: *Snapshot Replication, Transactional Replication* and *Merge Replication.*

- ***Snapshot* replication**: With this type of replication, the entire data set is replicated at each programmed time interval. The subscriber servers [servers that will replicate and make the changes to the other servers participating in the replication] are updated with an exact copy of the data published by *Publisher, with* no distinction being made between data that has been changed or not.

In this type of replication, the servers don't need to monitor the updates and don't control the changes, leaving a large amount of data to be transmitted between the servers, thus congesting the networks.

- ***Transactional Replication***: In this type of replication, only the changes made to the publisher are replicated to the subscribers. Any change made to one or more articles in a publication is immediately captured by the transaction log and replicated to the distributor, and this update is almost instantaneous.

The main advantage is the reduction in server update latency time, requiring servers with more memory resources for processing internal control agent updates.

- ***Merge Replication***: Its main feature is that changes can be made to any of the data replicas. Changes made to one of the replicas will be passed on to the others, converging on just one database.

This chapter has dealt with forms of Redundancy and their characteristics, which are necessary for understanding how *clusters* can be implemented, content covered in chapter 4.

CHAPTER 4

CHARACTERISATION OF THE *CLUSTERS*

The aim of this chapter is to present the main concepts of *clusters* and their classifications.

4.1 *CLUSTERS*

A cluster is a system comprising two or more computers or subsystems (called nodes), which work together to run an application or carry out specific tasks, in such a way that end users have the idea of a single, homogeneous system. Communication is done through *polling*, which are continuous requests for information, letting a server know that there are other *cluster* nodes in operation (ROCHA, 2004).

According to Backer (2000) *apud* Rocha (2004), *clusters* have certain criteria so that their structure has security, a defined standard and a purpose. To this end, certain requirements are made for their development and configuration, maintaining a single standard between the nodes that make up the *cluster*, the Operating System and the *hardware* configuration.

- **Application Purpose**: *Clusters* are used for high-performance processing or high availability of applications;
- **Node utilisation**: *Clusters* are dedicated when their processing is only being used to run certain types of specific applications. Non-dedicated clusters are used when the workstations are utilised for individual use and parallel applications are only processed when the system is not being used by users;
- **Node *hardware***: A node *hardware* structure can be made up of several computers (where each node can be a personal computer), i.e. several workstations;
- **Node Operating System:** There are several operating systems that can be used to create a *cluster,* among them the most widely used are *Linux* and *Windows Server. Linux* has advantages in terms of stability, flexibility and robustness, as well as low cost. On the other hand, *Windows* administration and management are very intuitive, and the system installation and configuration processes are automated.
- **Node Configuration**: In homogeneous *clusters*, all the nodes in the system have similar architectures and the Operating System is the same. Heterogeneous *clusters* use computers with different architectures and different operating systems.

The use of *clusters* can invoke characteristics such as Transparency, Scalability, Reliability, Management and Maintenance.

- **Transparency**

The *cluster* must present itself as a single system, i.e. the integration of distributed processing must be clear and efficient, regardless of which system is operating, in order to provide a given service (High Performance and/or High Availability).

- **Scalability**

The most important practice in terms of scalability is the transparent addition and removal of nodes within the *cluster. It* must be possible to add components to the *cluster* without interrupting the availability of active services, for example: adding nodes, peripherals and making network interconnections.

- **Reliability**

It is an analysis of the failures that can occur during its life cycle, and is not measured solely by failure calculation, but by the history of failures during its time in operation.

Some factors can interfere with the varying reliability of equipment, such as ambient temperature, humidity and previous maintenance. The *cluster* must be able to detect faults within the group and take action to prevent them from jeopardising the services offered.

- **Management and Maintenance**

Mechanisms must be in place to allow easy management, given the complexity of configuring and maintaining *clusters*.

4.2 GENERAL *CLUSTER* CLASSIFICATION

According to Pitanga (2003), there are some well-known types of *clusters,* among which are the *Failover Cluster*, High Availability Cluster, Load Balancing Cluster and Homogeneous and Heterogeneous *Clusters.*

- *Cluster Failover*

According to *Technet, Microsoft* (2013), the *failover* process is the *cluster* recovery model. This process can be understood as switching, through transactions, to an alternative node or a *backup node,* due to a simple failure situation in one of the *cluster nodes*.

The *failover* process must be completely transparent and automatic, without the intervention of a computer system administrator and, above all, without the need for the client to manually reconnect to the critical application.

For some non-critical applications that can withstand a longer time to recover from the failure, manual *failover* can be used. In addition to the time between the failure and its detection, there is also the time between detection and restoring the availability of the application and the resources involved in the computer system.

Large databases may require a considerable amount of time to adjust their tables. During this time the application will not be available.

To *failover* a critical application, the *cluster* nodes involved in using this mechanism must have equivalent resources. A resource can be a network communication interface or a disc, where the data on the disc is necessary to provide a certain service for the critical application in question.

Depending on the nature of the application and the computer system, executing a *failover* means interrupting transactions in progress, losing them and having to restart them after the *failover*. In other cases, it just means a delay until the application and the services available through the application are available again.

According to *Technet, Microsoft* (2013), the reverse process of *failover* is called *failback* and basically consists of moving the critical application and its clients back to the original node/server completely free of defects, errors or failures. Like *failover, failback* must be transparent and automatic for clients.

Failover can be used for another important purpose: maintaining the original node/server of the critical application. Simple, routine actions, such as updating the operating system or other *software*, and especially adding or maintaining *hardware* in the computer system, can be carried out without the need to stop supplying the critical application's services and resources. In some cases, due to the possible new interruption in the provision of the services involved in the computing environment, the *failback* process may be unattractive.

Depending on the application used, the *failover* method may or may not be efficient. Once the failure has been resolved, the server will make the service available and then you have the option of carrying out the *failback* process.

Figure 2: Before and after *failover*.
Source: (http://redes-e-servidores.blogspot.com.br/2011/09/failover-clustering-iv.html).

- High Availability *Cluster*

Used in tasks that require total system availability, where failure is insignificant, as any failure can cause serious damage to the end user.

According to Simões (2003), a High Availability *Cluster* includes two or more machines that are configured so that if one machine (or application) has problems, the second machine takes over the workload of both machines.

Each of these machines is called a high-availability node in the *cluster*. The High Availability *Cluster* is typically used in an environment that must be available, for example, a banking system where customers must call continuously. Figure 3 illustrates a High Availability *Cluster*.

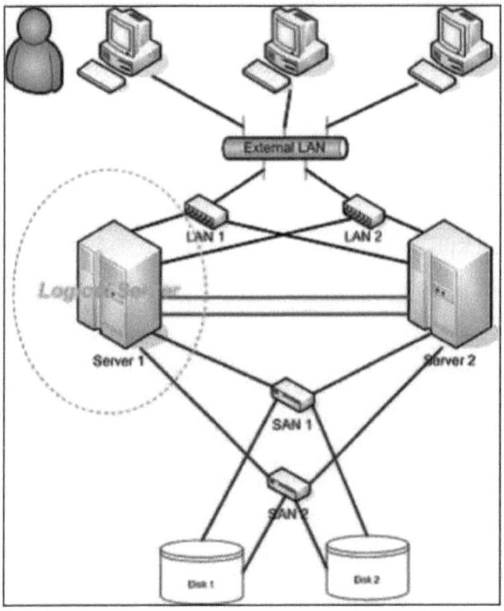

Figure 3: High Availability *Cluster*.
Source: (http://en.wikipedia.org/wiki/File:2nodeHAcluster.png).

To create a High Availability environment it is important to consider items such as the configurations needed to achieve High Availability, *Hardware* Redundancy and primary and secondary nodes, which would be like mirrors of the primary node.

Secondary nodes (or so-called mirror nodes) must have a consistent state with the primary (or mirrored) node, in terms of the data and/or resources involved in the service being offered (TORRES, 2003).

To build a *cluster*, you don't just have to think about a bunch of machines connected to each other, you have to think about its internal structure, the role that these machines will have to play.

High Availability *clusters* are divided into two types: symmetrical and asymmetrical. In symmetrical *clusters*, as illustrated in figure 4, the nodes work as if they were individual machines. Each server is configured to run an application, and there is no possibility of a server being on *standby*. In the event of a failure, the node in operation will take over the role of the failed node (FERREIRA and SANTOS, 2005, p.152).

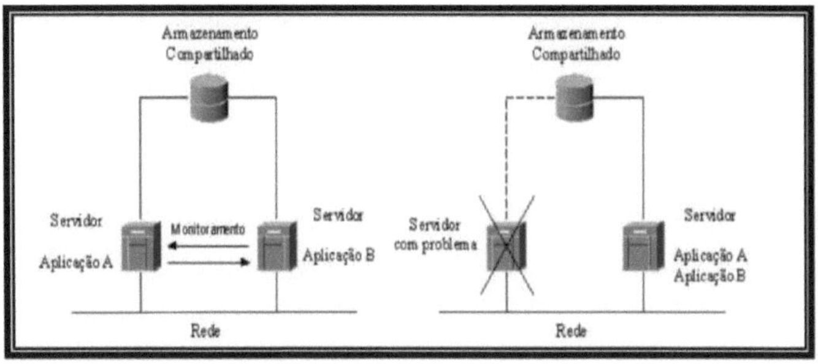

Figure 4: Symmetrical *Cluster* Type.
Source: (SIMÕES and TORRES, 2003).

There are disadvantages to using a symmetrical cluster, such as the difficulty of managing and securing the *cluster*. The distribution of jobs can be a problem, making it more difficult to find optimal performance.

The asymmetric *cluster* architecture, shown in figure 5, is more common. Applications run on the main server, with a redundant server in case of failure, initiating the *failover* process.

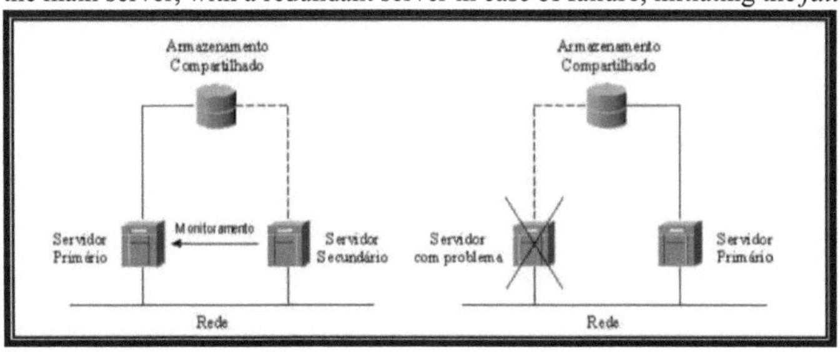

Figure 5: Asymmetric *Cluster* Type.
Source: (SIMÕES and TORRES, 2003).

The main disadvantage of this architecture comes from the limitations set on the performance of the main node. The main server must have high performance, as its limitations arise as the *cluster* grows. The way to solve this problem is to add servers within the *cluster*.

- **Load Balancing *Cluster***

According to Oliveira (2005), the purpose of this type of *cluster is to* distribute activities among the nodes. Through a load balancing algorithm, tasks are distributed among the system's nodes, resulting in a considerable improvement in performance.

It is used when a service is requested by many users and there are several machines responsible for responding to the same service.

To ensure that all machines receive an equivalent workload, *daemons* (monitoring programs) are active on each server, monitoring CPU utilisation and other resources. With the results of the monitoring, the servers are able to redistribute the workload, balancing the utilisation of all the servers.

If a node fails, the requests are redistributed among the available nodes. A Load Balanced *cluster is* highly scalable and can be easily expanded by adding new nodes. Figure 6 shows the Load Balancing *Cluster.*

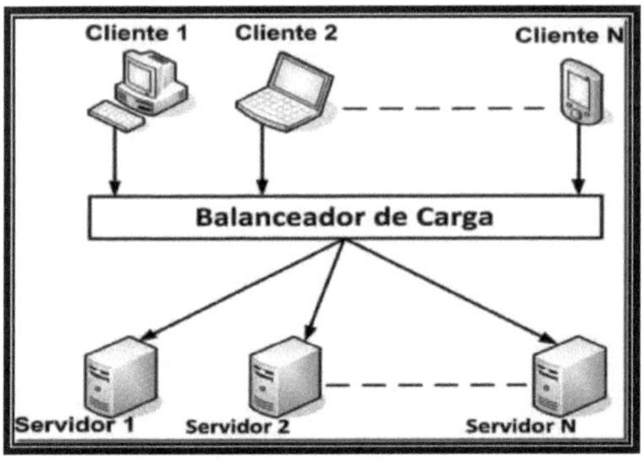

Figure 6: Load Balancing *Cluster.*

Source: (http://redes-e-servidores.blogspot.com.br/2011/03/balanceamento-de-carga-i.html).

- **Homogeneous and Heterogeneous *Clusters***

Homogeneous *clusters* have nodes composed of the same architecture and the same Operating System, so they understand the same instructions without the need for data transformation, in order to enable them to be processed on different processors. They are becoming a standard in the area of high-performance *clusters* because they are simpler to operate and do not present problems linked to data conversion between different Operating Systems and architectures (BACKER, 2000).

Heterogeneous *clusters* are those where the nodes they form have different processors and possibly different Operating Systems. They require data conversion so that an instruction can process on different processors.

According to Backer (2000), when new nodes are added or old nodes are replaced or repaired, the *cluster* can become moderately heterogeneous. One example is when components with a different year of manufacture, such as the CPU, are added.

When a *cluster is made* up of a mixture of different *hardware* and *software* components, it can potentially be heterogeneous in the long term.

The theoretical framework covered so far has been necessary to understand how a high availability solution can be implemented using proprietary *software,* as will be discussed in the next chapter.

CHAPTER 5

DEVELOPMENT OF THE *FAILOVER CLUSTER* IMPLEMENTATION

Based on bibliographic content and experiments already carried out using virtual machines, it was possible to verify excellent results with the implementation of the *Failover Cluster, which* can offer improvements to infrastructures that use centralised servers. The aim of this chapter is to carry out a detailed implementation of a High Availability solution applied in a corporate environment.

5.1 DESCRIPTION OF *CLUSTER* IMPLEMENTATION

This work has described step-by-step the configurations and installations of the functions and resources used by the servers during the implementation of the *Failover Cluster*. When one of the servers becomes unavailable, this implementation will reduce the downtime of the *hardware* and *software*.

The proposed study was not a simulation, but an implementation in a real environment with a contingency plan to improve the performance of the activities of a critical system.

The purpose of the implementation was to keep the resources installed on the servers and their applications available to users, even when there is some kind of interruption to the systems due to an unexpected event, such as natural disasters, *hardware* or *software* failures.

According to the objectives proposed in this work for the implementation of the *cluster*, the purpose was to inform the user that there is not just one server, but actually two servers working as if they were one, thus increasing performance, scalability and high availability.

Initially, it was necessary to map out the components and resources that would be used in the implementation, as well as to analyse the availability domain in order to know which data and services should be available to the application. Next, sufficient redundancy was added to these components so that failure situations could be circumvented.

The strategy for applying this procedure was to *failover* the affected resources, i.e. to dynamically reconfigure the *cluster so that* it could continue to provide its basic services and make application data available.

5.2 DESCRIPTION OF THE PHYSICAL ENVIRONMENT

The room where the servers are stored measures approximately 6 metres, with an air-conditioned environment. The servers are accessed from a *rack,* which is connected to a stabilised electrical network using 7,500W and 3,500W *nobreaks*, with 220V input and 110V output, whose function is to guarantee minimum unavailability in the event of an interruption in the power supply.

The corporate environment where the *Failover Cluster* was implemented has a fleet of thirty *desktop* computers.

These computers are interconnected by a *Gigabit Ethernet* network, which offers high performance and low latency with better scalability via a 3Com model 2952 manageable *switch* with 48 ports, which uses Category 6 network cabling. This *switch* connects and distributes the *Internet* to the active components that make up the network structure. According to figure 7.

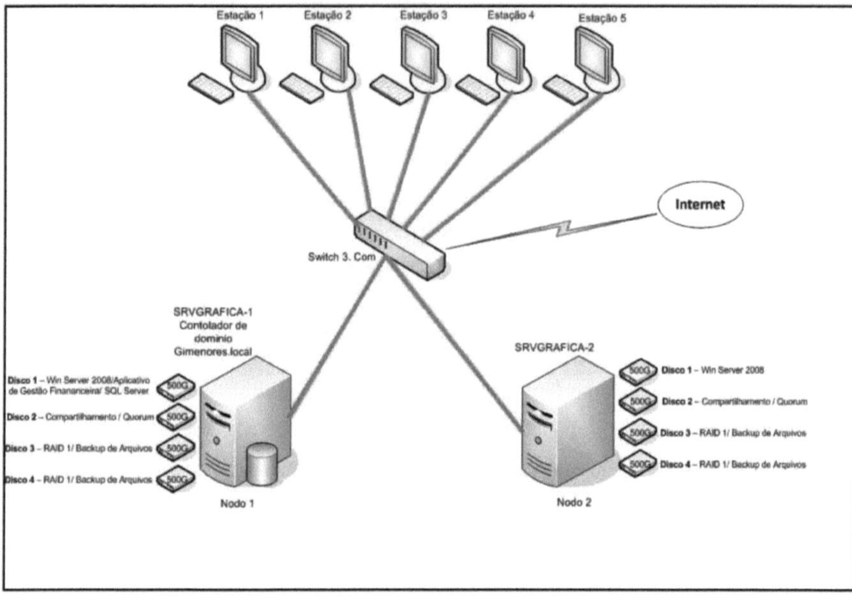

Figure 7: Corporate Environment Computer Park
Source: Author.

5.3 DESCRIPTION OF SERVERS

Two DELL computers with the following configurations were used: *Intel Xeon* CPU 2.40GHz processors, 8Gb of RAM memory, 4 (Four) 500Gb HDDs of storage space.

The servers used have redundant *hot-plug* power supplies (technology that allows devices to be connected while the computer is on without having to restart it).

Table 1 below shows the redundant *hardware* and some of the *software* used by the servers.

Table 1: Redundant server *hardware* and *software* configurations.

SERVERS	SRVGRAPH-1	SRVGRAPH-2
OPERATING SYSTEM	*Windows Server 2008 Enterprise R2 SP1*	*Windows Server 2008 Enterprise R2 SP1*
DATABASE	*SQL Server 2008 Enterprise R2*	
RAID SUPPORT	Integrated SAS 5/I controller	Integrated SAS 5/I controller
NETWORK	2x Broadcom NetXtreme 5721, *Single Port, Gigabit Ethernet,* PCI-E	2x Broadcom NetXtreme 5721, *Single Port, Gigabit Ethernet*, PCI-E

DISC PERFORMANCE	7200RPM	7200RPM
ENERGY SOURCE	2x670W *Hot Plug*, redundant power supplies	2x670W *Hot Plug,* redundant power supplies

Source: Author.

The SRVGRAFICA-1 server is the domain controller (gimenores.local) and manages all AD (*Active Directory)* users, which is a directory service implementation that stores information about computer network objects and makes this information available to users and network administrators. Some restriction rules are also applied to users through the use of group policy objects (GPO).

This server manages and stores the data and has a corporate application. This application has the functions of managing production information and financial operations, which are installed on the SRVGRAFICA-1 server, which has a *SQL Server* 2008 database server with *Enterprise* version.

There is a second server, SRVGRAFICA-2, which has the same *hardware* and *software* configurations, but there is no database or application installed, so it is not managing or storing data from the corporate environment.

The function of this server is simply to manage an industrial machine via a specific application on the machine itself.

The aim was to place it, as a child domain, in the same domain as the SRVGRAFICA-1 server. This procedure was carried out as follows:

J Advanced system settings;

J System properties;

J Computer Name;

J Change the computer's name or change its domain.

The implementation of the Operating System and Database *Failover Cluster* applies the rules for replicating the information contained on the SRVGRAFICA-1 server. This guarantees the availability of data and applications, ensuring *hardware* and *software* redundancy when failures occur. But for this implementation to be successful, the same applications had to be installed on the SRVGRAFICA-2 server.

5.4 DESCRIPTION OF THE LOCAL NETWORK

The *Internet* bandwidth used by the local network is 2 Mbps, provided by an ADSL connection linked by a *D-Link* model 500B modem.

The network structure is based on TCP/IP, as it uses the standard protocol for IPv4 networks, which makes it easier to deploy the *cluster*.

In order to manage and apply certain rules to the network structure, the corporate environment relies on the *Gatepro firewall,* which uses the *Linux Red Hat* Operating System version 5.1, whose function is to play the role of a *gateway,* which secures the content accessed by users, performing routing, VPN services and bandwidth control, as well as preventing virus threats.

This device has two network interfaces, one for external access and one for the internal network. It has two different IP addresses, one for the *Internet* and one for the internal network.

The ranges of these IP addresses are added to the external and local network interfaces as follows:

J The external network interface uses the IP 187.5.222.168/24.

J The internal network interface uses the IP 192.168.1.200/24.

The IP addresses of the SRVGRAFICA-1 and SRVGRAFICA-2 servers are shown in table 2 below.

Table 2: Server network address configurations.

SERVERS	INTERFACE-1	INTERFACE-2
SRVGRAPH-1	192.168.1.100/24	192.168.1.110/24
SRVGRAPH-2	192.168.1.150/24	192.168.1.155/24

Source: Author.

To implement the *Failover Cluster, it was* necessary to configure the two network interfaces of each of the servers. The addresses mentioned in the table above were configured before the *cluster* was built, as the IP address of the second interface of the SRVGRAFICA-1 server is the IP 192.168.1.110/24 called *host/domain*, which must already be defined with the domain name, resources and *failover* functions.

5.5 DATABASE STRUCTURE

The database used on the SRVGRAFICA-1 server is *SQL Server* 2008, which is installed in a centralised architecture, made up of a collection of 250 tables and containing 2,893,285 records, as well as other defined objects, including: views, indexes, stored procedures, user-defined functions and triggers to support the execution of activities with the data.

The data stored in the database is related to a particular subject or process, such as: stock information for production warehouses, financial transactions, customer and supplier registration information and the production of service orders.

In order to maintain the security and integrity of the information, this database is *backed up on a* daily basis. The main aim of this process is to provide a suitable and efficient environment for recovering, storing and guaranteeing the high availability of the information stored by distributing the data between the servers.

It is proposed to install and configure *failover* in *Windows* and *SQL Server* in SRVGRAFICA-

1 and SRVGRAFICA2, as this implementation will eliminate the problem of a single point of failure, an inherent characteristic of databases with a centralised structure.

5.6 FUNCTIONS AND RESOURCES INSTALLED ON SERVERS

The SRVGRAFICA-1 server was used as node 1, which acted as the domain controller. It was responsible for replicating the Database and Operating System information to the SRVGRAFICA-2 server, which acted as node 2 and was responsible for copying all the information inserted, altered and deleted from Server 1's Database.

The replication time of the information between the servers was configured instantaneously, i.e. synchronously, so that if one of the servers failed, the active node would take over and continue to be available to users without them realising that a failure had occurred.

When one of the servers becomes unavailable for some reason related to the database, its information may become out of date due to the synchronisation of the servers. Replication applied asynchronously will ensure that the server that was unavailable (*offline*) due to a failure event will receive the updated information after synchronising with the active server. This will happen once the problem has been solved and it is available again (*online*).

Before starting to install the resources, it was necessary to disable the *Windows firewall* on each of the servers via the control panel, as enabling it caused problems during the installations of some of the servers' native resources.

The process of installing *Cluster Failover* on the servers was done via the *Windows Server* Manager. After accessing the manager, the .NET *Framework* was selected for the installation of *Cluster Failover*, which is a resource that has the necessary functions for running programmes under any *Windows* Operating System, as shown in figure 8.

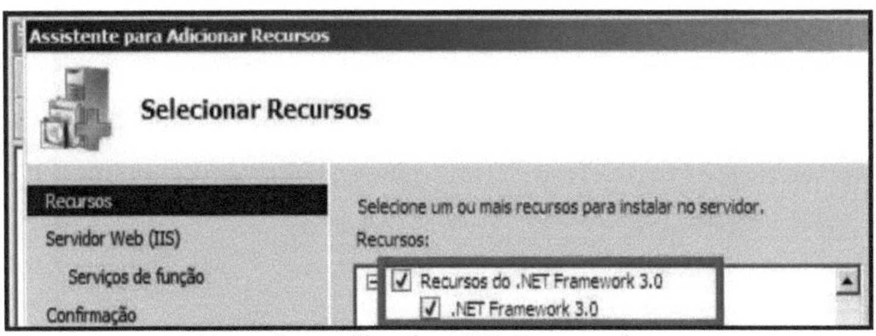

Figure 8: Installing the .NET *Framework*.
Source: Author.

5.7 IMPLEMENTING THE *FAILOVER CLUSTER* ON THE SERVERS

Failover Clustering is used for file, print and database services, as this group will keep a copy of the information that is part of the *cluster* on the servers. When a node fails due to an unexpected event, the active server will make a request to the group and start providing application availability. Figure 9 shows the period when the *Failover* Cluster was installed, whose function was to allow several servers to work together to provide availability of resources and applications.

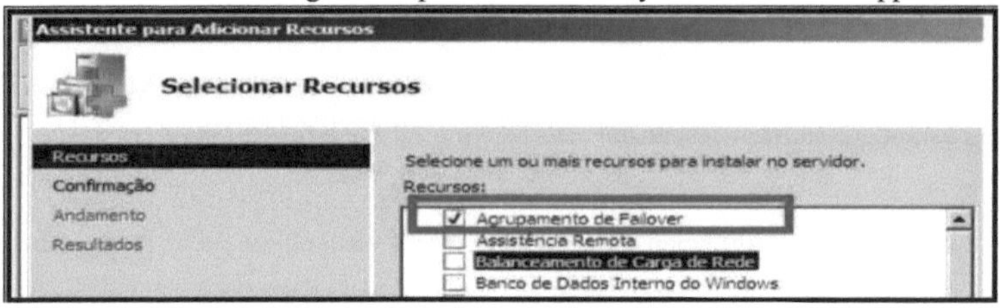

Figure 9: Installing *Failover* Clustering.
Source: Author.

This installation of the *Failover Cluster* is very important for the continuity of future installations, as it is necessary for creating and configuring the *cluster*. Figure 10 shows the formation of the new SRVGRAFICA-1 *cluster*.

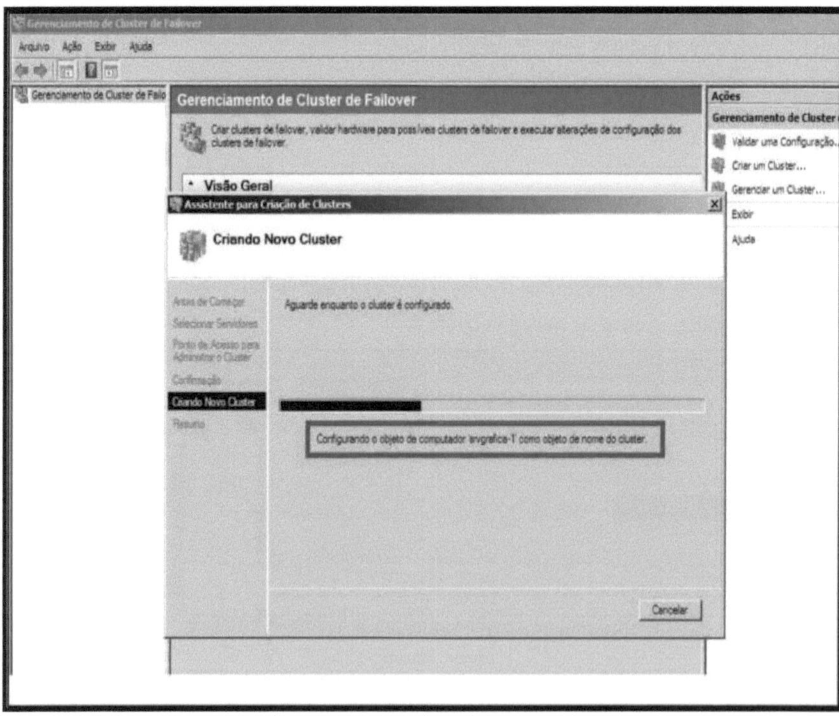

Figure 10: Formation of the new *Cluster*.
Source: Author.

Figure 11 shows the completed *cluster* formation stage, where all the SRVGRAFICA-1 server configurations can be identified via the manager.

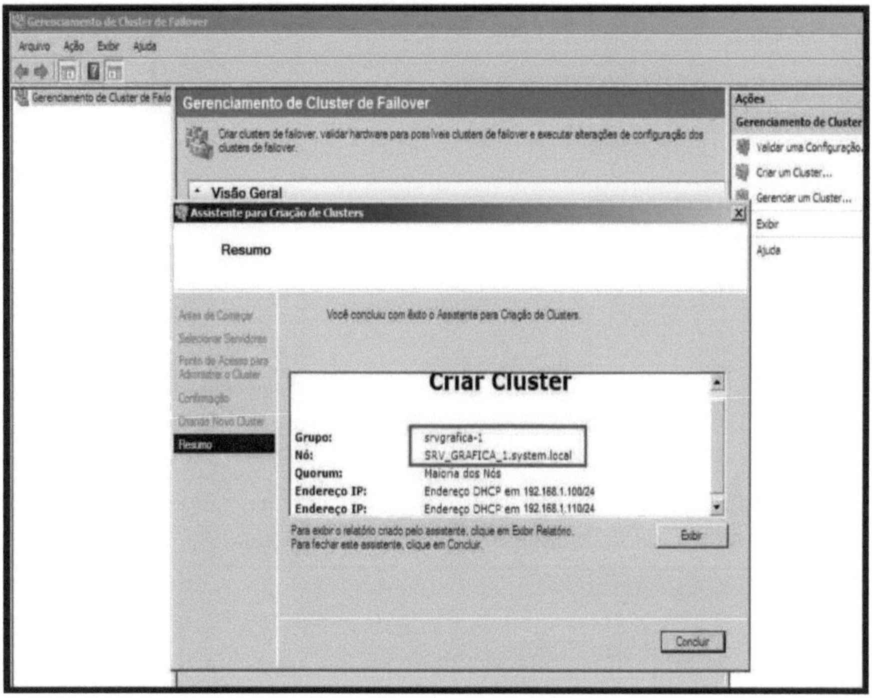

Figure 11: *Cluster* formation completed.
Source: Author.

5.8 IMPLEMENTING *CLUSTER FAILOVER* ON *SQL SERVER*

In order to maintain the same database configurations as the SRVGRAFICA-1 server, *SQL Server* 2008 *Enterprise had* to be installed on the SRVGRAFICA-2 server, as it did not have any type of database installed.

Figure 12 shows the completed *SQL Server* installation on the SRVGRAFICA-2 server, showing several steps that were successfully processed.

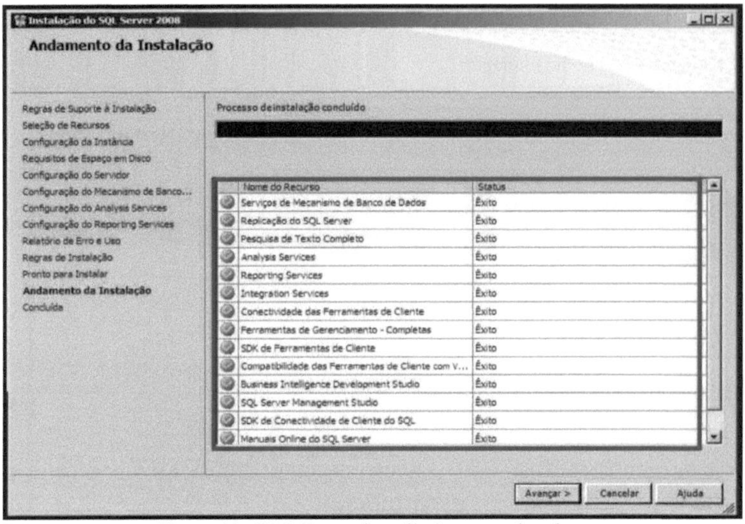

Figure 12: *SQL Server* installation completed.
Source: Author.

After completing the previous step, the *SQL Server Failover Cluster* was installed identically on the SRVGRAFICA-1 and SRVGRAFICA-2 servers, as shown in figure 13.

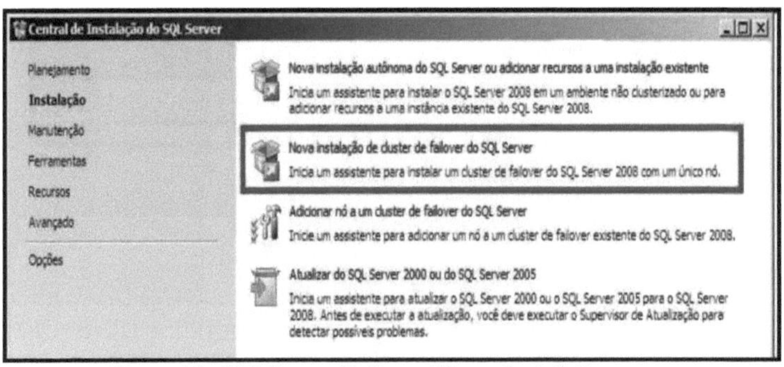

Figure 13: *SQL Server Failover Cluster* Installation.
Source: Author.

During the new installation of the *SQL Server cluster* on the servers, a problem occurred in the analysis of the processes executed, thus preventing the implementation from continuing, as shown in figure 14.

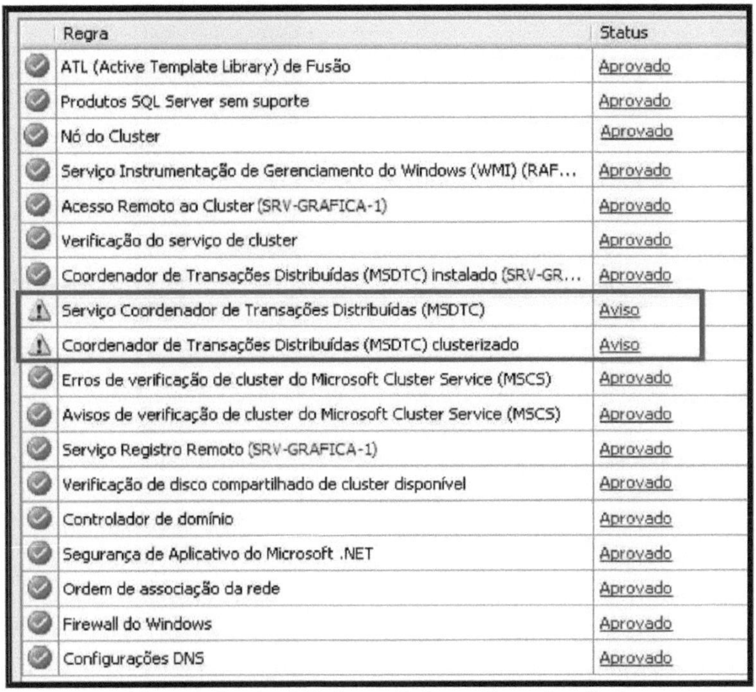

	Regra	Status
	ATL (Active Template Library) de Fusão	Aprovado
	Produtos SQL Server sem suporte	Aprovado
	Nó do Cluster	Aprovado
	Serviço Instrumentação de Gerenciamento do Windows (WMI) (RAF...	Aprovado
	Acesso Remoto ao Cluster (SRV-GRAFICA-1)	Aprovado
	Verificação do serviço de cluster	Aprovado
	Coordenador de Transações Distribuídas (MSDTC) instalado (SRV-GR...	Aprovado
	Serviço Coordenador de Transações Distribuídas (MSDTC)	Aviso
	Coordenador de Transações Distribuídas (MSDTC) clusterizado	Aviso
	Erros de verificação de cluster do Microsoft Cluster Service (MSCS)	Aprovado
	Avisos de verificação de cluster do Microsoft Cluster Service (MSCS)	Aprovado
	Serviço Registro Remoto (SRV-GRAFICA-1)	Aprovado
	Verificação de disco compartilhado de cluster disponível	Aprovado
	Controlador de domínio	Aprovado
	Segurança de Aplicativo do Microsoft .NET	Aprovado
	Ordem de associação da rede	Aprovado
	Firewall do Windows	Aprovado
	Configurações DNS	Aprovado

Figure 14: Problems during the *SQL Server Failover Cluster* installation.
Source: Author.

This problem could have been caused by reasons such as iSCSI card failures, a network node failure or the Operating System. This problem was identified through the servers' system event *logs*.

In this case, the problem occurred because the MSDTC (*Microsoft SQL Server* Distributed Transaction Coordinator) was not running. To activate this process again, it was necessary to install an update to a package called *hotfix,* which has the function of carrying out various *software* repairs while the system is running, i.e. while the system is switched on.

After this correction, the server was restarted and the SQL Server *cluster* installation was run again, where the installations for each *cluster* were analysed and processed, and the configurations were carried out at the same time, as shown in figure 15.

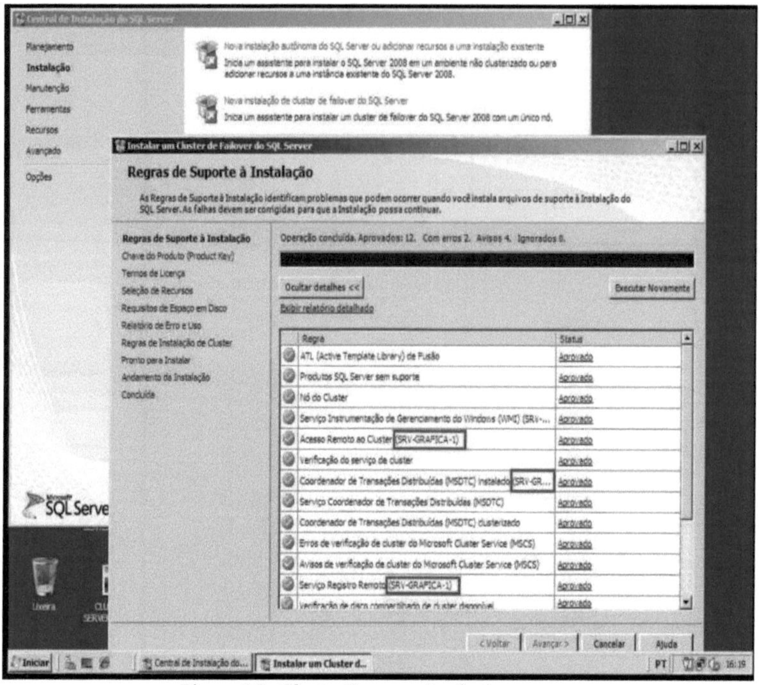

Figure 15: *Cluster* Process Analysis.
Source: Author.

5.9 CONFIGURING DATABASE REPLICATION

Once all the database installation and configuration processes had been carried out and the *SQL Server cluster* had been created, *the* type of replication to be adopted for these databases was defined.

For this case, we opted for Asynchronous Replication, which will replicate the 250 database tables, and any information changed in the tables will be propagated and applied to the other database server, even if it is temporarily out of synchronisation. But when synchronisation takes place with the server that has become unavailable *(off-line)*, it will send the data to all the specified locations.

After defining the type of Replication that had been applied, it was necessary to configure the local publications and subscriptions of the SRVGRAFICA-1 and SRVGRAFICA-2 Database servers.

When *SQL Server* was installed on the SRVGRAFICA-2 server, the metadata that makes up its logical and control structures was configured. Among these metadata, the most important structures are: *Master, Model, Tempdb and Msdb*. This metadata is part of the Database Management System.

The Distributor was created on the distribution server when the Replication process was configured and is used to store the histories of the transactions to be replicated.

It was also necessary to define the Distributors and Publishers of the transactions in the Databases. In this case, it was decided that the two servers would have the role of

Distributor/Publisher. A Distributor/Publisher server is responsible for distributing and storing metadata and historical data for all types of replication.

Servers that only have the function of publishers include tasks that allow users to add content to a report server. Figures 16, 17, 18 and 19 below show the main configurations made.

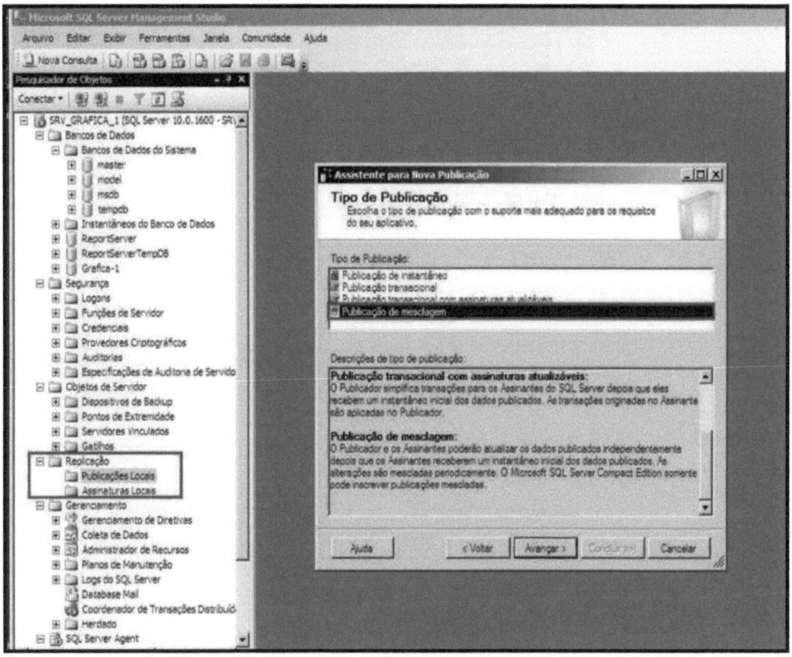

Figure 16: Installation of Merge Publishing.
Source: Author.

In this type of merge publishing, which was applied to the servers, the SRVGRAFICA-1 Distributor/Publisher, as well as the SRVGRAFICA-2 server, updated the published data independently after receiving an initial snapshot of the published data.

Changes will be merged periodically according to the availability of each server. This procedure can be changed or defined in the publication installation itself. In this case, all the tables in each database have been selected to be replicated from one server to another.

When choosing the items to be published and replicated, you can specify which schema objects should be copied to the servers, as declared referential integrity. This can include primary key restrictions, reference restrictions, unique restrictions, indexes, user DML triggers, extended properties and groupings.

The extended properties are only replicated in the initial synchronisation between the servers. Figure 17 shows the Publishing process.

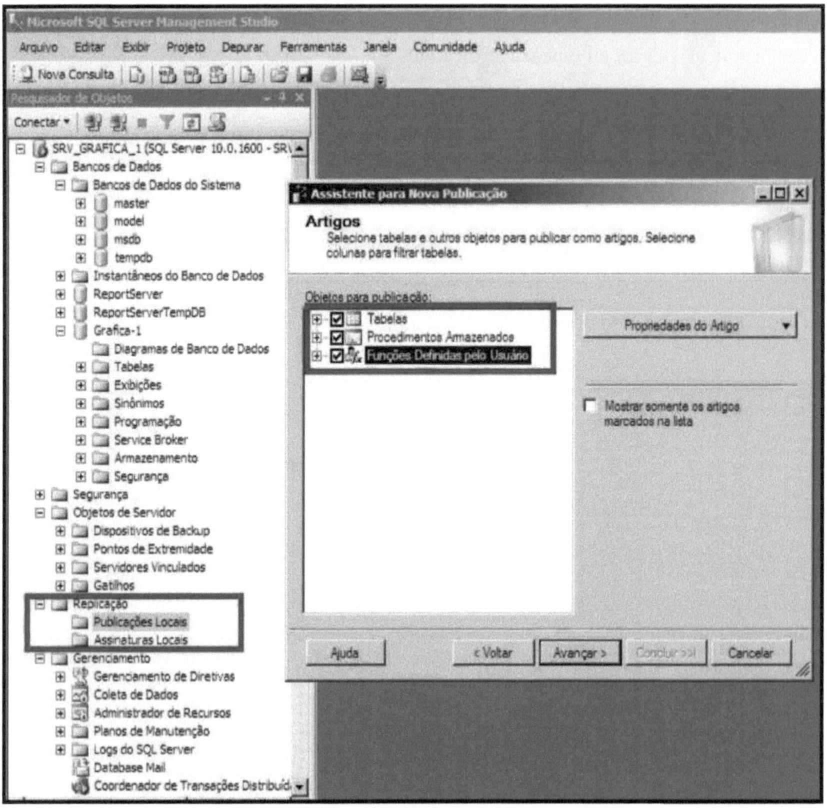

Figure 17: Publishing the database tables.

Source: Author.

After defining the data to be published and replicated from one server to another, the Distributor/Publisher server analyses the selected items and if there are no problems, the publication is completed, as shown in figure 18.

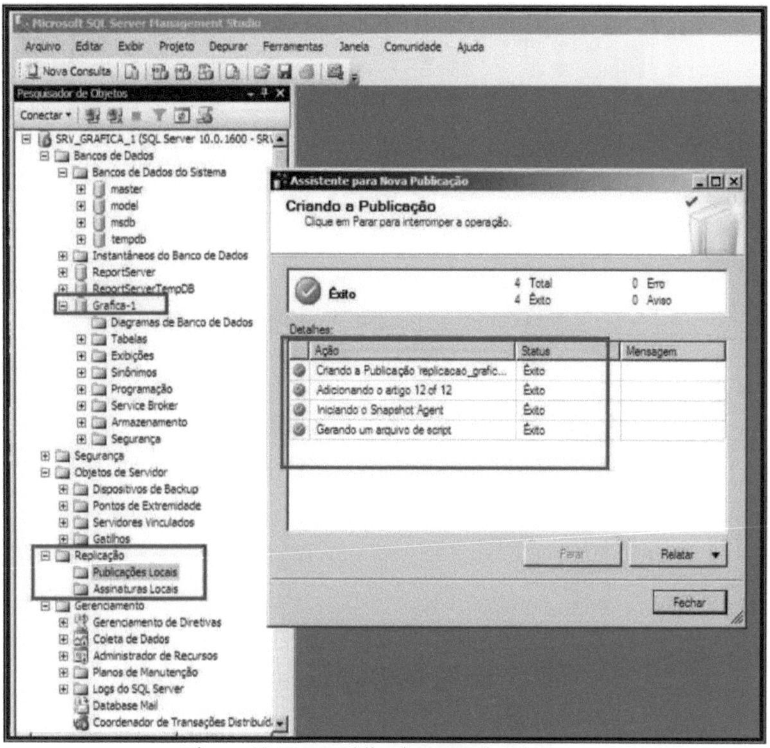

Figure 18: Data publication completed.
Source: Author.

The subscription created on the SRVGRAFICA-2 server is a request to obtain a copy of the data and Database objects in a publication that was made on the SRVGRAFICA-1 Distributor/Publisher server. Situation shown in figure 19.

This subscription defined which publication was used, where and when it was received, according to the items previously selected in the publication.

To plan this subscription, we considered where the agent processing should take place. To do this, the subscription type that controlled the agent's execution location was executed on the two servers, SRVGRAFICA-1 and SRVGRAFICA-2. The Merge or Distribution Agent was executed on the Distributor itself. See figure 19.

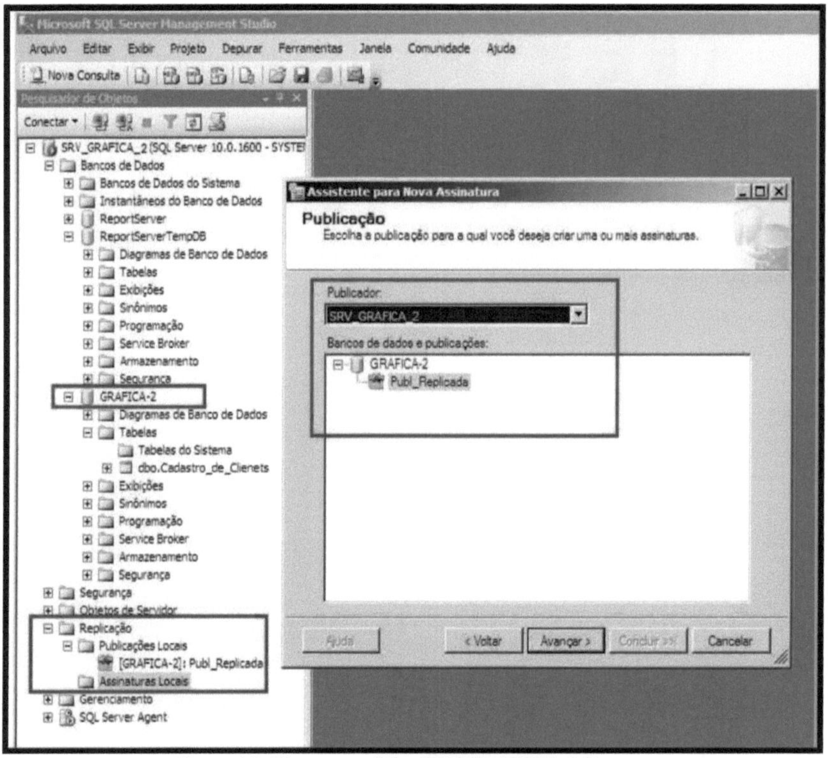

Figure 19: Signature of the SRVGRAFICA-2 Server.
Source: Author.

This chapter has described step-by-step the installations and configurations for implementing the *Failover Cluster*. These actions were necessary to carry out the experiments and collect the analysed data in order to answer the research problem and objectives proposed in this work.

CHAPTER 6

EXPERIMENTS AND DATA COLLECTED

Throughout the theoretical framework studied, no rule or pre-requisite was identified that addressed a pattern or sequence for carrying out tests with *Cluster Failover*. Therefore, in order to collect the results obtained with the implementations, this work did not adopt any type of rule or sequence of specific tests to be carried out.

To analyse the performance of the implementation, native tools that were pre-installed on the servers and *software* provided by the manufacturer were used.

The first tool used to test the *cluster* was the *Windows MMC* (*Microsoft Management Console*), which is the File Server Resource Manager. This tool is a resource that has various services and manages the applications installed on the operating system.

Figure 20 identifies all the implementations carried out on each server, in this case SRVGRAFICA-1 and SRVGRAFICA-2, as well as the Operating System cluster configurations, the *SQL Server cluster* configurations and the replications defined. At the same time, another resource was run, the *cluster*'s High Availability Wizard, where it was possible to visualise the applications.

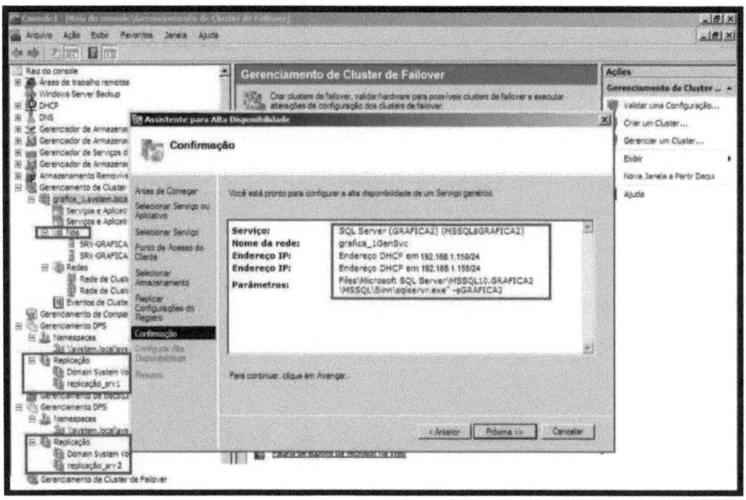

Figure 20: Implementations and Confirmation of the *Cluster*'s High Availability.
Source: Author.

After this procedure, another very important test was carried out. The *cluster* validation tool was run using the *Failover Cluster* Manager, which analyses all the *hardware* and *software* configurations implemented on each server.

Thus, it was possible to identify all the processes executed and analysed by the *cluster*'s Validation Assistant, where there were no restrictions on the previously configured implementations

(Figure 21).

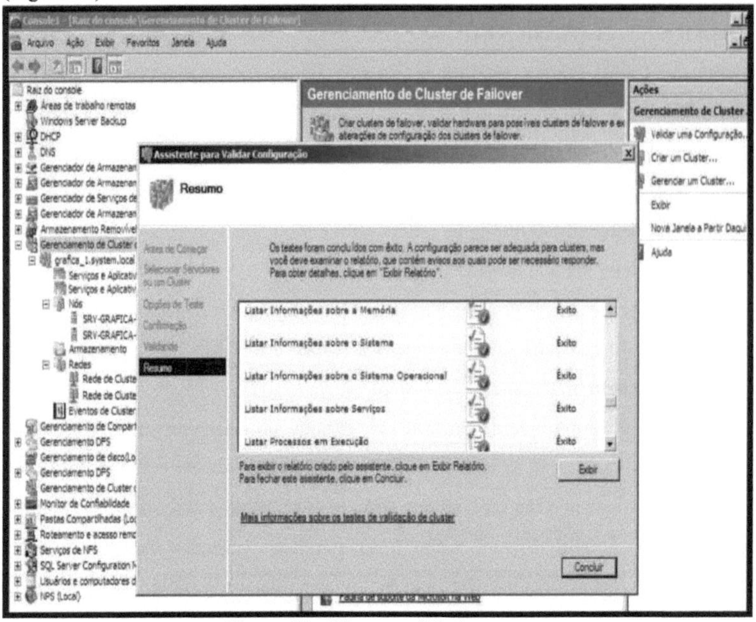

Figure 21: *Cluster* validation.
Source: Author.

After completing the previous tests, one of the servers was disconnected by unplugging the network cable from the interface. This process could also have been carried out by switching off the power or by simulating a database failure.

The server was disconnected while one of the databases was being updated. This procedure was carried out on purpose to check and test the *Failover Cluster* and also to see how the replication would behave after the failure.

The server that was undergoing the database update was SRVGRAFICA-2. As it had previously lost connection, the SRVGRAFICA-1 server automatically took control of all the services that were being provided by server 2, but the database update was not replicated due to the network failure occurring at the same time as the update. Despite this, all the applications were available to users without them realising the failure of one of the servers.

Figure 22 shows via the SRVGRAFICA-1 server's *failover cluster* management tool that the SRVGRAFICA-2 server is unavailable (*offline)* on its network interface and has failed to replicate to the Database.

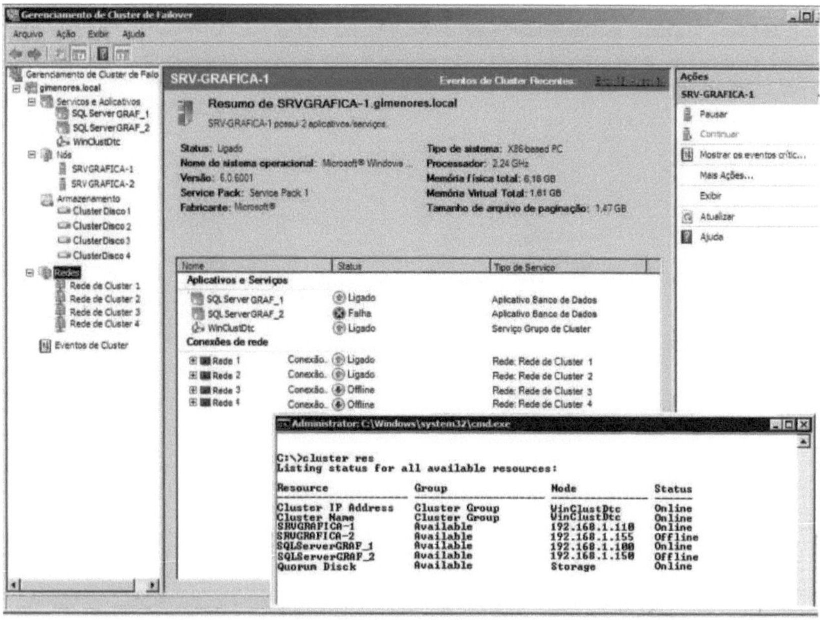

Figure 22: Failure of the SRVGRAFICA-2 Server.
Source: Author.

The fact that the replication procedure did not take place at the time of the failure did not interfere with the operation of the SRVGRAFICA-1 server, as it already had the necessary information from the database to make it available to users.

The SRVGRAFICA-2 server was disconnected for five minutes, which was enough time to analyse the behaviour of the *cluster* and its results. Figure 23 shows how the *failover* procedure works.

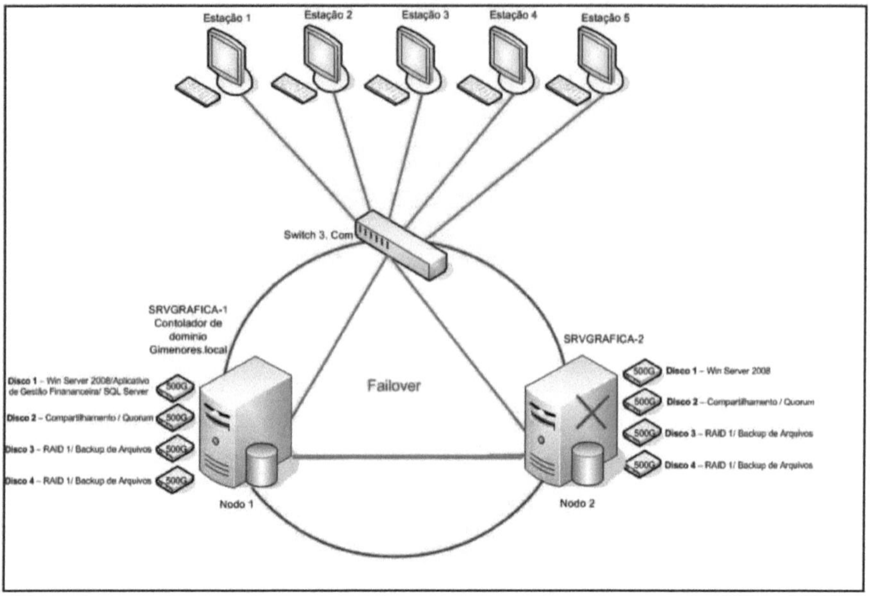

Figure 23: When the *failover* takes place.
Source: Author.

After this time the server was disconnected, the network cable was plugged back into its interface, where it was possible to analyse via the server's *cluster* management tool that all the SRVGRAFICA-2 processes had been re-established.

The update that was taking place when the SRVGRAFICA-2 server was disconnected was transmitted after it was actively synchronised *(online)* with the SRVGRAFICA-1 server, as shown in figure 24.

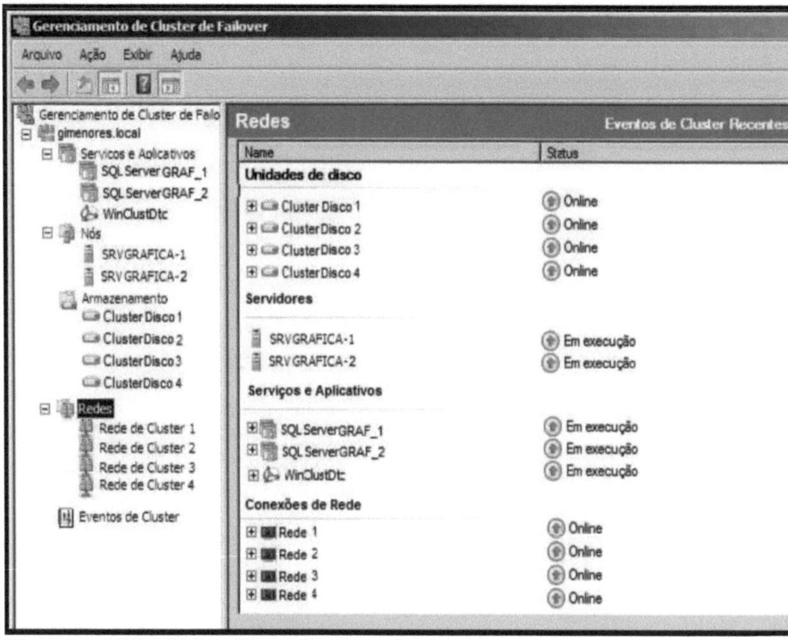

Figure 24: All the *Online Cluster* Services after the tests.
Source: Author.

After synchronising and updating the servers, three packages were *downloaded: SqlCmdLnUtils_x86.msi, SharedManagementObjects_x86.msi,PowerShellTools_x86.msi*[1] .

These packages are tools that use *scripts to* help with the *Benchmark* technique (the act of running a computer program, a set of programs or other operations in order to evaluate the performance of a process), which installed together will partially evaluate the performance of the Databases.

These packages were very important for understanding how the databases would respond under varying conditions.

Using these packages, scenarios can be created that evaluate the handling of *deadlock* [blocking], application performance, different methods of loading data, transaction rate characteristics, how many users are added and the effect on the application.

The packages were installed and run on the SRVGRAFICA-1 and SRVGRAFICA-2 databases in order to evaluate the response time performance of each of these servers.

The figure below (figure 25) shows the time each process takes in milliseconds. These packages use scripts that execute the commands within each Database: *Creating Table, Writing Data, Updating*

---

1 ________ . Available at: < http://www.microsoft.com/en-us/download/details.aspx?id=30440>. Accessed on 15 July 2013.

Data, Reading Data, Deleting Data and Dropping Table.

The function of each process performed is table creation, data writing, updating, reading, data deletion and table deletion. These commands showed the response time for each operation, so that the performance obtained by each database could be analysed.

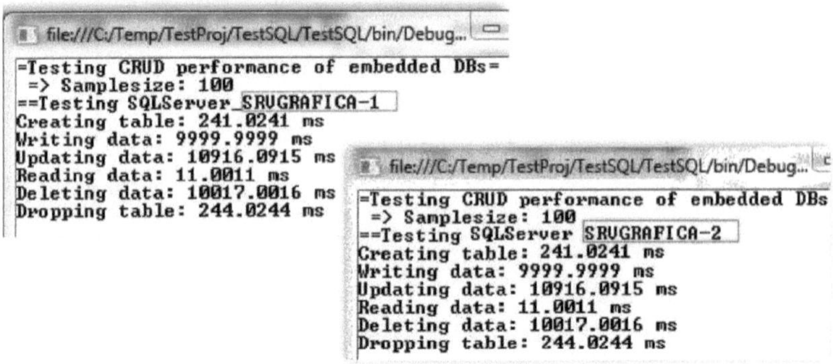

Figure 25: Response time for each server.
Source: Author.

To analyse the results of the performance evaluation of the processes executed in each database, a graph is generated with the data obtained by the packages, which identifies that there are no differences between the processes.

This means that all the operations performed in the figure above (create, write, update, read and delete) are at the same time interval, with the same level of response time performance, as shown in figure 26.

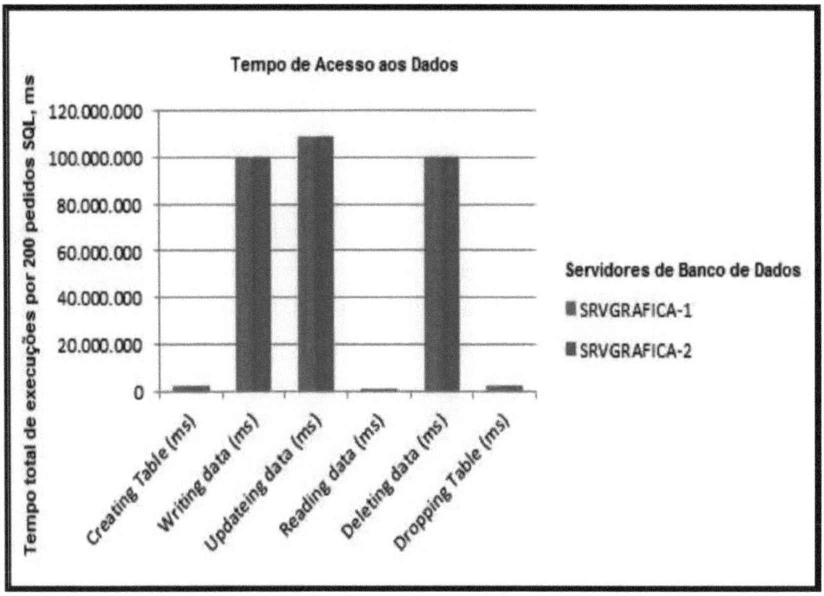

Figure 26: Analysis of processes carried out on servers.
Source: Author.

The graph above shows a comparison of the processes carried out between the servers, where the response time for each operation carried out was the same for each server. This procedure showed that the *SQL Server Failover Cluster delivered the* expected results in terms of server response time performance.

In obtaining the results, according to the tests presented above, it was possible to make adjustments to the *cluster*'s configurations, such as controlling the configurations, identifying errors, failures or possible problems before they cause a period of inactivity.

CHAPTER 7

CONCLUSIONS AND FUTURE WORK

During the course of this work, steps were taken to install and configure a *Failover Cluster.* To evaluate the tests, we used tools native to the Operating System itself and others that were installed, as described in the previous chapter.

The *Failover Cluster* Verification/Validation tools evaluated the following items: Storage: where the *cluster*'s discs, file system and disc access latency were validated; System Configuration: all system *drives, Active Directory* settings and *software* updates were validated and checked; Inventory: where all information about system *drives, software* updates, BIOS information and running processes was listed; Network: where network communication, *cluster* nodes, IP addresses and *Windows firewall* settings were validated and tested.

After the previous tests, the following tools were used: *SqlCmdLnUtils_x86.msi; SharedManagementObjects_x86.msi and PowerShellTools_x86.msi,* installed to evaluate and compare the performance of each server's *SQL Server Failover Cluster*. They executed commands for creating tables, writing data, updating, reading, deleting data and deleting tables. A graph was then generated with the data obtained to compare the performance of each server. It was found that the two database servers have the same performance.

It was possible to analyse that the objectives proposed by the work were achieved, but the objective of testing the performance of the systems was partially achieved, because there are more tests that could be carried out. The servers responded to the tests applied, thus guaranteeing the availability of data between the servers and their applications. Organisations that rely on this type of implementation have more secure data, since having data redundancy is a factor that generates less costs.

As future work, we suggest a more in-depth study of the subject, thus expanding the possibility of carrying out more scientific work that requires an environment of this size to generate significant data, such as using more tests to evaluate the performance of the systems. The architecture developed in this study can be used to encourage new configurations for using the *Failover Cluster*. The implementations and tests applied in this work could be carried out using other operating system and database platforms.

REFERENCES

ALECRIM, Emerson. ***Clusters*: Concepts and Characteristics**. Available at: <http://www.infowester.com/cluster.php>. Accessed on: 23 June 2013.

ASWINI, A.A.; MANISANKAR, V.R.; JAGADEESAN, J. ***An Efficient Approach For Avoiding Down Time Of Production Data Base Server In Active/Passive Windows Failover Clustering Environment.*** International Journal of Innovative Technology and Exploring Engineering (IJITEE), V.1, N.3, 2012 .

BACKER, M. ***Cluster Computing White Paper***, Final Release, Version 2.0, University of Portsmouth, UK, 2000.

DATE, C. J. **Arquitetura a Sistemas** de **Bancos de Dados**. p8. ed. Rio de Janeiro: Campus, 2004.

FERREIRA, Filipa Silva; SANTOS, Nélia C. Gaspar. **High Availability is divided into two types: Symmetric and Asymmetric,** Instituto Leira, Politécnico de Leira, 2005. 152p.

FREITAS, F. (2003) and BRAGA (2001). **Data Replication** . In: Renata Vieira; Fernando Osório. (Org.). Proceedings of the XXIII Congress of the Brazilian Computer Society. Volume 8: Mini-Courses in Artificial Intelligence. Campinas: SBC, 2003,v. 8, p. 1-52.

LAUDON, K.C. LAUDON, J.P., 2004, **Management Information Systems**. 5. ed. São Paulo, Prentice-Hall Inc.

LOPES, Léo. **Data replication using *SQL Server* 2008**. Available at: < http://www.blogdati.com.br/index.php/2011/07/replicacao-de-dados-utilizando-sql-server-2008/ >. Accessed on: 20 Apr. 2013.

MELO, 1997, **Banco de Dados**. r. 2. ed. Rio de Janeiro, Livraria e Editora Infobook S. A, 2004.

NUNES, Paulo. ***Benchmarking***. Ed. São Paulo: Sistema *on-line* de Gestão Empresarial magazine, 2008. Available at: <http://www.knoow.net/cienceconempr/gestao/benchmarking.htm>. Accessed on: 20 Apr. 2013.

OLIVEIRA, Leonardo R. **Analysis of Fault Tolerance and Load Balancing**, Bachelor's Degree in Computer Science, Course Conclusion Work - TCC, Salvador, UCSal, 2005.

OLIVEIRA, Daniel Cândido. **Development of a High Performance Cluster,** Dissertation (Conclusion of the Discipline - Practical Information Systems I), Palmas, ULBRA, 2004.

PEREIRA FILHO, Nélio Alves. **Relevance Services for High Availability Clusters,** Master's Thesis, São Paulo, 2004.

PITANGA, Marcos J. **Computação em *Cluster*.** 1. ed. Brasport, 2003.

ROCHA, Lidiane Lins. ***Cluster*** - Overview, Article, Brasília: UCB, 2004.

SILBERSCHATZ, A.; KORTH, H.F. ***Database System Concepts.*** 2. ed. Singapore: Ed. McGraw Hill, 1991.

SIMÕES, Eduardo Issi; TORRES, Guilherme Mundim. **High Availability Server *Clusters*.** Final Project, Goiânia, UFG, 2003.

SHOMAN, M.L. ***Probabilistc models for Software Realiabibity Prediction***. Ed. Academic, 2002.

TECHNET, Microsoft. ***Failover and Failback.*** Available at: <http://technet.microsoft.com/en-us/library/cc757139.aspx>. Accessed on: 20 April, 2013.

TECHNET, Microsoft. ***Cluster Failover.*** Available at: <http://technet.microsoft.com/pt-br/library/cc731844%28v=WS.10%29.aspx>. Accessed on: 27 April, 2013.

WEBER, Taisy Silva. **Fault Tolerance: Concepts and Examples**. Postgraduate Programme, UFRGS, 2002.

WEBER, T.;Jansch-Pôrto, I.;Weber, **Fundamentos de tolerância a falhas**.Vitória: SBC/UFES, 1990. (handout prepared for the IX JAI - Jornada de Atualização em Informática, at the X Congress of the Brazilian Computer Society.

TANENBAUM, Andrew S. ***Computer Networks.*** 4 ed. Rio de Janeiro: Editora Campus, 2003.

VOLLERTT, João Rosaldo. **Reliability and Field Failures: A Case Study for Improving Product and Repair Reliability Through a Systematic Data Collection Procedure**. Postgraduate Monograph, Santa Catarina, UFSC, 1996.

ZHANG, R., ABDELZAHER, T. F., and STANKOVIC, J. A. 2004. ***Efficient TCP connection failover in web server clusters***. In Proceedings of the IEEE InfoCom Conference. Vol. 2, 1219-1228.

MIX
Papier aus verantwortungsvollen Quellen
Paper from responsible sources
FSC® C105338

Printed by Books on Demand GmbH, Norderstedt / Germany